FOR GIVE:
Stories of Reconciliation

Lou Ruoff

RESOURCE PUBLICATIONS, INC.
San Jose, California

Editorial director: Kenneth Guentert
Production editor: Kathi Drolet
Copyediting, layout, and production: Elizabeth J. Asborno

Reprint Department
Resource Publications, Inc.
160 E. Virginia Street, #290
San Jose, California 95112-5848

Library of Congress Cataloging in Publication Data
Ruoff, Lou, 1946-
  For give : stories of reconciliation / Lou Ruoff
     p.   cm.
  ISBN 0-89390-198-9
  1. Reconciliation– Religious aspect s –Christianity–
Meditations. I. Title. II. Title: Forgive.
BV4509.2.R864 1991
242– dc20   90-29144

7 6 5 4 3 l 98 97 96 95 94

Excerpts from the New American Bible with Revised New Testament, © *1986 by the Confraternity of Christian Doctrine, Washington, D.C., are used with permission.*

The epigraph on page v is reprinted with permission from Storytelling: Imagination and Faith, © *1984 by William J. Bausch (paper, 232 pages, $7.95) published by Twenty-Third Publications, P.O. Box 180, Mystic, CT 06355.*

To Anna and George,
my parents,
who took me as their own.

The spirit of the LORD shall rest upon him:
  a spirit of wisdom and understanding...
Then the wolf shall be a guest of the lamb,
  and the leopard shall lie down with the kid;
The calf and the young lion shall browse together,
  with a little child to guide them.
The cow and the bear shall be neighbors,
    together their young shall rest;
    the lion shall eat hay like the ox.
The baby shall play by the cobra's den,
  and the child lay his hand on the adder's lair.
There shall be no harm or ruin on all my holy
  mountain;
for the earth shall be filled with knowledge of the
  LORD,
as water covers the sea.

Isaiah 11:2,6-9

...telling one's story is to open oneself to self-discovery.

This self-storytelling becomes an essential process in finding God. People will match their stories against his, especially against the Jesus story. This is why a person's story has become a critical factor in the new Rite of Christian Initiation for Adults. When someone inquires about becoming a Catholic, it is first necessary to share one's own personal journey and the most important events in it. This sharing leads to questioning, to a search for meaning to the person's story. In turn, this leads to a reflection on the stories of faith. In this inquiry the person tries to see if the Jesus story throws any light on his or her own...Personal storytelling is the context for discerning God's activity and presence. In self-discovery one is likely to discover God as well.

William J. Bausch,
Storytelling: Imagination and Faith

Contents

■ *Acknowledgments*

In my first book, I thanked a number of people and parishes. They served me well with love before and since, and my love for them continues. But there are others I want to thank for being there, in love, for me, as I to them:

Ralph and Connie Celli,
Ed and Katherine LoBello,
Larry and Pam Gardner,
Steve and Tamara Higgins,
Frank and Dolores Wagner,
David and Janice Drexler,
Jack and Agnes Phillips,
Phyllis and Jack Cannon,
Vickie and Carlton Hubbard,
Joey and Mary Kozak,
Pat Pratali,
Cathy Griffin,
Skip and Jan Rawls,
Bobby Taylor,
Maureen and Don Story,
George and Teresa Pelbano.

And my priest support group:
> Jay Biber,
> Paul Maier,
> Walter Barrett,
> Tim Drake,
> Tom Miller,
> Greg Dodge,
> Charlie Ferry,
> Kay Morhard.

And the entire community of St. Richard Church, Emporia, Virginia. And to George and Dorothy Daly, who contributed greatly to the viability of this small parish community.

One half of all profits from the sale of this book will go to Homeless Haven, a shelter for Norfolk's people of God who are without a place to stay.

The other half of all profits will go to Norfolk's Catholic Worker—again, a place of Christian hospitality serving God's poor and needy.

For Give

■ *Woman in Sin*

What do you suppose Jesus is ready to tell the
woman who is about to be stoned by a mob here in
John's gospel? It is the
> cry of every child
> and of every young adult;

it is the wish of every parent; it is the most sought-
after expression ever devised by human mind. If we
listen, listen ever so carefully, with our eyes closed,
we can almost hear
> that cry,
> that wish,
> that expression

on the lips of Jesus as he approaches the woman: "I
understand." Have you ever noticed Jesus never
points his finger at any sinner?

He doesn't condemn.

He doesn't insult.

Jesus never dwells on the faults and weaknesses of sinners; rather, he cares for them. Jesus loves his people; his people are precious to him for they are his Father's creation.

In all of Jesus' action, the only people who come under his flaming wrath are those who feel they are too good to be sinners; those who feel they are better than others. Now, we know who they are: the self-righteous who are always scanning someone else and forgetting—or worse yet ignoring—their own person.

When Jesus speaks those soothing words, "I understand," he challenges us, challenges us to grow and change. It is a challenge that leads to maturity and spirituality.

And when we (here tonight) hear those words "I understand" and accept the challenge, our lives will be
> more focused,
> more in tune,
> more goal-filled

with the spirit of life as never before. I would like to tell you how I was challenged by those words "I understand." I was challenged by a Jesus figure during my first year at St. Mary's Seminary in Baltimore. The person's name was Denis O'Callaghan, a priest who was my advisor for four years at the seminary. (Denis, by the way, died the Christmas of '85.)

During my many conversations with Denis, I had shared my past as honestly as my mind could recall. Denis, for his part, listened well; he heard all I was saying.

3

The challenge came one afternoon when all the theology students were packing their gear to leave the seminary for Christmas. Knowing I was without a car, Denis offered me a ride home; besides, he was heading in the same direction.

When we finally arrived at my house after an exhausting three-hour ride, I got out of the car and readied myself for the usual slamming of the door and a hearty "thank you" when Denis' stern voice blurted out, "Well, aren't you going to invite me in?"

I was afraid to.

I was afraid because my home was a house where yelling and screaming was as natural as if it were a stadium; where insulting names were thrown around as if it were a playground; where tears were as common as a losers' locker room. During my teenage years, my relationship with my parents was very strained at best, destructive at worst. Now I couldn't allow Denis in to see how my mom and I interacted. What would he think of me? Could I ever confide in him again? With all that in my mind, I invited Denis in.

After forty-five minutes with my mom and me, Denis left the house, and as I was walking him to his car he must have noticed
> my discomfort,
> my embarrassment,
> my anger.

No one was saying anything:
> he stopped,
> I stopped,

4

he looked at me and said, "I understand." Those words of Denis' were a comfort to me at that moment. Those words were like a cool gust of wind on a smoltering, sticky summer night.

I invited Denis into my house that day because of trust. Are we going to trust Jesus enough to invite him into our hearts?

(Tonight) Jesus,
              in the form,
              in the image
of the Church and its ministers, is saying to each of us as we prepare for individual confessions, "I understand."

■ Judas' Betrayal

Palm Sunday   *Matthew 26:14-25*

Crying is so emotionally cathartic and so spon-
taneous that at times people shy away from crying
people because they are uncomfortable. But other
people, often enough, tend to extend themselves to
those shedding the tears.

It sometimes happens that joy overwhelms us and
tears of joy cannot be contained. But more often
than not, tears come from pain and hurt—even self-
disclosure. Our emotional need is to express ourselves, and the most common, and perhaps the best,
way is for us to cry.

Jesus cried at the tomb of his dead friend Lazarus.
Peter, as well, wept—wept bitterly when he realized
he had denied his Master. Legend tells us that to the
day of Peter's death, marks of his tears were visible
on his face.

They say crying cleans things out of the system; all
that is trapped inside comes out—all for the good!

I'd like to share a story with you.

Just recently a ten-year-old girl came up to me at my church's communal reconciliation service. I noticed her hesitation as she approached—more exactly, I saw the tears that were welling in her eyes. I reached down to meet her. As I did, the tears began to flow from her eyes.
>I did what came naturally to me;
>I wiped the tears from her eyes.

As the little girl shared with me what she wanted God to know and forgive, tears continued to flow. Wiping her eyes, I placed the tears in the palm of my other hand until a very small puddle appeared. I asked the girl
>to see herself in that puddle,
>to see her sincerity, her sorrow,

and then I asked her to continue on her journey in life where she will meet many people with tears in their eyes, and that her ministry/duty in life will be to wipe away the tears from others.

This incident brought me back to the day, many years ago, when I was about thirteen. My new parents brought me into their home,
>gave me a new identity and roots,
>gave me the family I had never
>experienced before.

During the course of my first year with my parents, I betrayed their trust. I took silver coins from the cookie jar my parents had stashed away in the kitchen cupboard. Taking the coins was a way for me to make friends so that my new neighborhood

wouldn't seem so foreign to me. I wanted to be accepted. Buying things for the neighborhood guys
> got me noticed,
> got me the attention

I craved—but I was just fooling myself.

When confronted by my mom, I denied it totally. She told me that my father, the disciplinarian, would take care of me when he came home from work. Waiting on the living room couch for six hours for dad to come home still brings terror to my mind. I felt
> so embarrassed,
> so ashamed

of myself, I cried my eyes out. And when dad opened the door, I ran to meet him with tears streaming from my eyes. I confessed. I told him everything, fearing he would
> disown me,
> send me back where I came from.

But my dad did something unexpected. He hugged me tightly; he even thanked me for being honest and owning up to my responsibility. And then, he wiped away my tears. When my tears ceased, dad told me that my one dollar a week allowance would continue—but that I would know what to do with it. And for the next fifty weeks or so, I placed my allowance into the cookie jar.

These examples remind us of Judas' betrayal.

We know that Judas was
>> so embarrassed,
>> so ashamed of himself,
>> so guilt-ridden
that he went off and hanged himself.

Much as in our age, when teen suicide is so prevalent, Judas saw
>> no alternative,
>> no option,
>> no hope.
I am sure the little girl at the communal reconciliation had no understanding of the depth of her sensitivity, just as I had no understanding of how deep was my father's acceptance of me. I only wish Judas had allowed Jesus to see the tears in his eyes. I know what Jesus would have done.

(By the way, after our service all the participants had coffee and donuts at the church hall and I noticed the little girl running with other youngsters having a good time—a sort of human resurrection!)

■ *"He has gone to...the house of a sinner."*

31st Sunday of Ordinary Time (C)   *Luke 19:1-10*

(An) American businessman...(had) two dozen Soviet engineers in thrall. "It's important what you wear, because Americans make quick judgments about people..." *Newsweek* (December 25, 1989):71.

Do you remember when you were a youngster going through the funnies and finding a puzzle that stimulated your interest? Maybe you had to find ten things that were either missing or simply wrong in the puzzle—and you would spend the time and effort to find those things:

> Maybe an umbrella was missing as the father left the house into a rainstorm?
> Perhaps his shoe was missing?
> Was there a knob on the door?
> No steering wheel as the father goes to the car?
> A car with only three tires?

This kind of kiddie exercise was fun—is, even today, fun. But in today's gospel we have a picture, and there appears to be something wrong with the picture. But unlike the funnies, this isn't fun. Something is missing. What might it be? Perhaps rereading the gospel might help us?

The principles of our gospel are as follows:

Jesus

A man named Zacchaeus

A sizable crowd in the town of Jericho.

And the facts are these:

Zacchaeus wants to get a better look at Jesus and climbs a sycamore tree.

Jesus sees Zacchaeus, sees value in Zacchaeus, and invites himself to Zacchaeus' house.

Zacchaeus is "delighted" that Jesus sees fit to come to his house.

The crowd doesn't see value in Zacchaeus.

The crowd is displeased and resents Jesus' desire to go to a sinner's house.

Zacchaeus defends himself quite well.

Jesus accepts Zacchaeus' candor.

Now I don't know if eye glasses were around during the time of Jesus, but I think someone needs glasses to see better. Whether it is Jesus or the crowd, someone isn't seeing correctly. Who would it be that might benefit from having a pair of eye glasses?

If I can move away from our puzzle for a minute or so, I would like to share with you an experience I had last week.

Every week I visit people on death row at a prison sixty miles from where I minister. Having arrived, I saw a twenty-nine-year-old man in his cell. Noting that Christmas was nearing, I asked him, "If I could bring you something, what would you want?" "A pair of glasses," he said without any hesitation. Looking through the prisoner's cell slot with a bewildered look on my face, I said, "Glasses!?" The young man told me that his vision became severely impaired sometime when he was in the seventh grade. His vision was blurred, but he was too embarrassed to say anything because he was one of the ones making fun of others wearing glasses. The prisoner lamented, "Now that I have all this time on my hands, I need glasses to see and read..."

On my way home, I stopped at a nearby nursing home to see a seventy-nine-year-old woman. At one point during our conversation, I asked her the same question I had asked the inmate earlier, "What would you want for Christmas?" Without pausing to think, the elderly woman said, "Glasses." "Say again?" I asked, disbelieving what I heard. Calmly, she repeated, "Glasses."

I was somewhat stunned because she was already wearing glasses. When I questioned her why she felt she needed glasses when in fact she had glasses, she sadly said, "I really can't see that well; everything is blurry—even with my glasses on. I wear glasses because of habit; I haven't had an eye exam for some thirty years. I have all this time on my hands, and would like glasses so I can see better."

They tell us that in our society two thirds of all Americans wear/will wear corrective lenses. That's about 175 million people using modern technology so that they will see better!

Now back to our gospel picture and using glasses as a way to understand the scene better: Who do you think needs glasses? Might it be Jesus? Perhaps Zacchaeus? How about the crowd?

> Not Zacchaeus—because he has *insight* as to who Jesus is, and he *saw* correctly.
>
> Not Jesus—because he is the *light* who *saw* value in an otherwise despicable person; he is *light* that doesn't pass judgments on people in the same way people pass judgments on one another.

Is it the crowd? Yes, the crowd could have used plenty of glasses. But, do you think eye glasses would have helped the crowd anyway?

Do you think eye glasses might help you judge people better? I need corrective lenses. You think I'm wearing them—but I am not. The glasses you see on me, well, I'm taking them off and will crush them under my foot. There you see, no glasses to see now. But those glasses weren't mine. I obtained that pair from the Lions' Club.

The point is: You thought I could see, but in reality I couldn't.

Not all/every lens will work—only the "lens" Jesus gives us. Only by allowing our sight to be filtered through Jesus can we have *insight*. And only by allowing the *light* to dispel darkness and distortion, and illumine what we see will we ever *see* with the clarity of Jesus.

■ *Man Born Blind*

Jesus touched the multitudes. His ministry was a ministry of touching and healing.

Jesus touched
> the sick,
> the diseased,
> the demented,
> the lame,
> the blind,
> the lost and forsaken,
> the dead.

Peter's mother-in-law lay in bed with a severe fever. Her hand is touched—the fever vanished.

The leper approaches the Teacher saying, "You can make me clean." Stretching out his hand, the Teacher makes him clean.

After a deaf and mute spirit comes out of a boy and throws him to the ground, Jesus takes the lad's hand and raises him up.

A woman "completely incapable of standing erect," is set free of her infirmity when he lays hands on her.

Two blind men—their eyes touched—they see light again!

A sinful woman at his feet—comfort and mercy prevail!

He touches
>   in Jericho,
>   in Bethsaida,
>   in the district of Decapolis.

Ashore at Gennesaret they seek to touch his tassel— a woman does—and her hemorrhage is cured.

At Nazareth, in the synagogue, they shout: "What mighty deeds are wrought by his hands!"

When he touched and healed, there was rejoicing. Though not always; he encountered controversy.

He touched a man with dropsy and was cursed by
>   the Pharisees and
>   the scholars of the Law for not
>   following
>   the letter of the Law.

A little girl lay dead in her bed; he raised her up.

In the city of Nain, he touched
      a coffin,
      pieces of wood hammered together,
      once part of a tree
and a widow's son returns to life!

In the city of Bethany, He told those standing near a
cave, wailing, to move the stone sealing the tomb of
Lazarus. When they touched the stone (a stone
covered through the centuries with layer and layer
of volcanic ash, interbedded with shale, mud and
other earthly deposits) and moved it, Lazarus
walked out.
      "Alleluia!" they shouted.
      "Praise the God among us!"

In the city of Washington, he stands erect at
      a wall,
      a wall with names,
        just names;
      a black wall,
      a granite wall;
      a wall of confusion,
        of anguish,
        of pain;
      a wall of bitterness,
        of disillusionment;
      a wall filled with grand memories;
      a wall filled with mighty hopes;
      a wall filled with empty promises.
At the wall, he focuses his sight and thoughts on a
little boy of five upon a father's shoulders, touching
      a name,
      just a name,

of someone the father knew and loved—a buddy he knew in a war thousands of miles away and whom he misses.

At the wall, tears swell in Jesus' eyes at 57,000-plus names. He reads the names.
>Names.
>*Names.*
>Haunting.

At the wall
>he sees beyond the names,
>he sees identity,
>he sees
>family,
>co-workers,
>neighbors,
>acquaintances,
>people who will be affected for years
>to come.

He places his hand on the same name as did the little boy. With the father's permission, he touches the child's forehead. The father brought the boy down from his shoulders so that Jesus might bless the child. Indeed Jesus did with a kiss, hoping
>this boy,
>any boy,
>no one
would ever have to go to war in the future to kill
>anyone
>anymore.

■ *"That they may be one..."*

7th Sunday of Easter (B) *John 17:11-19*

When I was about seven years old and taking a shower with all the other youngsters (as was the custom in the orphanage every night), I remember being struck by something most unusual. The boy next to me had six toes on one foot! This youngster became somewhat uncomfortable, for he knew what I was doing and thinking. And when I looked at him for the first time in my life, I realized he was black. I had an immediate dislike for this person, which eventually grew into hatred.

That is how hate usually happens—something as innocent as having six toes. From our differences we develop distrust, division, separation, and hate. Though only seven, I could have learned much from the similarities each of us shared with one another; but that direction was somehow forgotten at this moment in my life, especially during these formative years.

The greatest of all similarities each of us share with one another is that we are precious people whom God created and loves.

I'd like to tell you a story about differences that led to division.

There were three families who lived one next to the other. They were the handsomest, happiest, most contented families anyone could hope to see. The families, whose names were the O'Malleys, the Goldbergs, and the Washingtons, were a credit to their community. They regularly volunteered their time and services to civic and religious functions. They were conscientious in all their habits, at home and at work. In fact, their examples were faithfully imitated by others who learned from them.

The O'Malleys lived in a green, split-level house; the Goldbergs lived in a red bungalow; and the Washingtons lived in a brown ranch-style home. Each of the families, amazingly enough, had one child: all boys, all the same ages.

One day, Sean O'Malley, who was seven years old, noticed Tyrone Washington had only four fingers while they were playing catch with one another. It bothered Sean, and after playing ball, he asked Tyrone why he had only four fingers while everyone else had five. Tyrone felt insulted and questioned why Sean had freckles when no one else had. Both children left disappointed with each other.

The next day, Sean decided to have a game of catch with Jacob Goldberg. Sean noticed Jacob had a rather large nose, which upset him to no end. Sean went home to report to his parents all that he had seen. The parents became upset and told Sean to look for other friends. Tyrone and Jacob also told their parents, and their responses were the same as the O'Malleys.

The very first Saturday after this incident all the fathers started erecting fences around their property. The fences were so high that no one could see inside, nor could anyone see outside. The mothers, for their part, began telephoning neighbors up the street, down the street, all across the city telling all about the crude people living next door to them.

The next day, being Sunday, the O'Malleys and the Washingtons went to their respective churches, and it struck each of them that the Goldbergs had gone to a synagogue on Saturday. This annoyed both the O'Malleys and the Washingtons because the Goldbergs lived right in the middle of them. Each of them started thinking, "We should have known better." While at church, God was telling the O'Malleys and the Washingtons the same words the Lord told the Goldbergs the day before: "I love you. I love *all* my people." But the families weren't listening to God, just complaining to God about the stinking neighbors next to them!

After their respective services, the O'Malleys remembered, somewhere back, long ago, that the Catholic Church was the only true church and all the others were make believe. This enraged Mr. O'Malley for he realized that not only were the Washingtons black, but Baptist as well. The Washingtons started feeling

21

much anxiety because not only were the Goldbergs Jewish, but the Washingtons were buying their home from the Goldbergs. The Goldbergs' frustration hit a high note when they realized their zoning permit to open a bagel shop had to be passed by city council, which was predominantly Irish and Catholic.

Each of the families took their feelings to the street: they bought guns and cannons and built bunkers for what they were calling an all-out war. It was unfortunate that in all the madness, no one took time to listen to that voice breaking through the clouds from the heavens:

I love you all,

each of you are members of my family.

Unfortunately nations behave the same as these children and their parents. Nations are made up of individuals.

Jesus gave all of us a challenge: to love one another. Jesus, however, did not stop there, he gave us the greatest of all challenges: Love our enemies.

If we truly love Jesus, there is no two ways about it!

■ The Question of Divorce

27th Sunday in Ordinary Time (B)   *Mark 10:2-16*

Divorce.

It's one of those losing propositions: if you take the side of one, you anger the other; if you side with the other, you hurt the one. It seems you cannot be neutral when a divorce hits
> people,
> family,
> home.

The Pharisees brought the question of divorce to Jesus' attention. We know the Pharisees were very calculating people, always looking to take advantage of an unsuspecting someone in order
> to test and
> to trick
that someone who's trying to follow God's way—a way not often in line with the self-appointed "in crowd."

As pertaining to the question of divorce, the Pharisees approved the dissolubility of the marriage commitment, and they wanted to track down and abuse Jesus, hoping to trap and trick him over his own words because he taught and preached the opposite. The Pharisees didn't just want to bring Jesus down, they wanted to make him a
>test case,
>show case,
>a prime example
to anyone who would dare disagree with them. They wanted to make a colossal fool of him.

Now, the Pharisees were cunning because they knew they had an ace up their sleeves. That ace was Moses. It was Moses who granted divorce petitions. Moses was revered throughout all Israel. To all good Jews, Moses was
>the great Prophet,
>the great Law-giver, and
>the great Leader
who led them to the Promised Land. And who would be so obstinate to quarrel with Moses? Certainly not Jesus, the Pharisees figured, despite the fact
>"this creep,"
>"this wack," and
>"this crazed one"
is going around telling people he's God's Son. Even he won't disagree with Moses, the Pharisees thought.
>They thought.
>They thought again.
They gambled their entire credibility on the question of divorce. The Pharisees ganged up on Jesus and

asked whether divorce was permissible. Remember, Jesus was no softy; rather he was confident when dealing with these scheming individuals because he also had an ace up his sleeve.

Jesus' ace was God. Jesus reminded the people that God allowed for union of man and woman and stated no one should separate what God had joined. And so Jesus turned the table and fired the question back to the Pharisees, "What command did Moses give you?" The Pharisees responded rhetorically, "Oh, Moses said it would be OK, didn't he?" Jesus replied, "Yes, he did." The Pharisees were grinning ear to ear when Jesus added, "That was because people like yourselves were selfish and Moses had to satisfy them. They were, like yourselves,

> self-centered,
> self-indulgent, and
> self-righteous."

"Self-righteous!?" the Pharisees vehemently protested while their grins gave way to frowns.

"Yes, self-righteousness."

The Pharisees represented the institutional Church of its time; they were unmoving and intolerable when human faults came up against the Law.

> Jesus' openness to sinners was
>   extraordinary,
> his compassion for sinners was
>   moving, and
> his love for people, realizing their
>   weaknesses was exceptional.

Perhaps our institutional Church of today can learn a lesson in our story, as we all can. The Church has, at times, been in the position of the Pharisees, clinging ever so tightly to the letter of the Law. In regard to the question of divorce, the Church has correctly stood up for the indissolvability of marriage, but at the same time, in many cases, refusing to acknowledge that judgment is not theirs alone.

Like the Pharisees, the Church, in some cases, has inflicted harsh judgment on people struggling to find a better,
> more spiritual,
> more productive,
> more mature, and
> more satisfying

way of life and commitment. And like the Pharisees, the Church, many times, never fully understands the consequences of their actions.

Many times, Jesus showed adults and institutions who the first ones are to suffer because of their actions—he brought before them a child.

When I was about six years old, after having lived in an orphanage from birth, a couple took me to their home for several weeks. This couple fell in love with me and I with them. They discussed with me the possibility of my becoming their child. It sounded great to me, but it never happened. Years later I was informed that one of the couple was a non-Catholic and thus was not permitted to adopt a Catholic child. That was a hard and fast rule in those days— as was the one about how a person seeking priesthood could not because a divorce in his family denied him that privilege; or the one about how the other person seeking priesthood could not because, since he was born out of wedlock, he could not even be considered for sacred ministry.

I suppose someone could have also said that to Jesus!

■ *"How many times must I forgive?"*

24th Sunday in Ordinary Time (A)   *Matthew 18:21-35*

There was once a sheriff who ruled timidly over a vast territory in a land called the badlands. It was called the badlands because of the crippling terrain, but also because love could not be found there. Suspicion and destruction of life were the order of the day. Many people inhabited this territory without any real choice of their own.

The sheriff loved the townspeople, though they didn't deserve to be so loved. The sheriff was getting old and tired. He had been around a long time; in fact, no one could remember a day he wasn't on the job. The sheriff was liked by the townspeople, but few took him seriously. This troubled the sheriff very much. Long ago he had made a promise to the people, and one day he decided to fulfill that promise. The sheriff decided his only son should take control of the badlands. The townspeople rejoiced, for they knew it would be business as usual, expecting "like father like son." They sang and danced. They didn't deserve to be so loved.

One day the son came into town, which was located not far from a river. His clothes were nothing out of the ordinary. His white hat sat neatly on his head. His first act was to go into the local saloon, where he chose twelve people to be his deputies. The son accepted an invitation to go to a wedding reception, where the townspeople could meet him. He ate a couple sandwiches, drank a cup of watered wine, arranged for new wine to be brought in, and left. The entire town noticed that he wasn't wearing a badge nor carrying a gun. They laughed. They didn't deserve to be so loved.

The people brought all their problems to the son—all their concerns and all their ailments. The son, with unusual power, saw to it that the people were taken care of. He saw to it that a new law

> of justice,
> of peace,
> of love

was incorporated into the town's by-laws. Some of the leaders, however, rejected the ways of the son.

> They were envious;
> they were conniving.

They didn't deserve to be so loved.

The son told them stories of hope and gave them his mercy and compassion. He even fed 5,000 people when the grocery store ran out of food. The son calmed several storms. He even found a lost sheep or two. But he wasn't welcomed into the churches of the badlands. Oh, they were all so cruel. They didn't deserve to be so loved.

Then one day, the son was arrested by the townspeople, on the charge of impersonating a sheriff.
>They whipped and beat him.
>They even spat in his face.

The townspeople strung him on a tree, like a convicted bank robber, and left him to die. Even his deputies ran away in fright. The son cried to his father, "Forgive them!" They didn't deserve to be so loved.

Death came.

The father arose from his rocking chair, stood up straight, crying as he did so, and screamed at the top of his voice: "Why?"

The father sat down and
>forgave them all,
>forgave all the townspeople.

They didn't deserve to be so loved.

The father welcomed the son home. He held a grand and wonderful banquet for him and invited everyone. Yes,
>*everyone.*
>Everyone from the badlands.
>*All* were invited!

Do they deserve to be so loved?

■ *Jesus Cures Deaf Man of an Impediment*

23rd Sunday in Ordinary Time (B)   *Mark 7:31-37*

Jesus
> cured,
> healed,
> relieved, and
> reassured

all the people who came to him with various ill-
nesses. No one was excluded—not the lame, nor the
blind, nor the down and out, nor the sinners, not
even the lepers. Now, this all took place in the town
of Tyre.

The news of Jesus traveled to Sidon, in the region of
the Ten Cities, where they were anxiously awaiting
his arrival. It so happened there was a certain
gentleman named, well, he could never say his name
completely because he stuttered and stammered so
badly that no one was able to understand a word he
would say; though the fact was no one would wait
around long enough to find out. After two thousand
years, wouldn't it be fitting and just to give this par-

ticular gentleman a name? What shall I call him? Why not Galilee, after the famous sea of Galilee?

The story that surrounds Galilee's stuttering and stammering was that when he was only four or five years old he went to the busy marketplace with his father, and while at that jam-packed market, Galilee witnessed an accident that took him completely by surprise. It upset and startled the child greatly. Galilee, quickly trying to catch his father's attention, which was momentarily diverted in another direction, excitedly screamed "D-d-d-d you-o-ou-ou s-s-s-see th-th-that?"

The father was horrified by what he heard. Oh no, not the accident; he was horrified by his son trying to speak in a way he had never heard before. The alarmed father berated the youngster with a harsh yell: "Listen to yourself! You're stuttering! You're stammering! Now stop it!
Stop it!
Stop it
this very instant!"

Unfortunately, Galilee's father, from that day on, never allowed the lad to forget his stuttering and stammering, and it stayed with him;
became part of him;
became his sole identity.

Galilee had a hard time adjusting to the behavior of those people who hadn't experienced someone stuttering and stammering in their presence. Brothers and sisters felt embarrassed when he was around and offered Galilee candy and sweets to stay away.

Playmates giggled and laughed nervously and offered to play hide and seek—and forgot to seek out
Galilee. Teachers sat Galilee in the back of class (out
of sight, out of mind) and recommended him for
remedial reading. Doctors threw their hands up as if
to say, there's nothing that can be done; he's
retarded; he's a menace to others—and offered to
quarantine Galilee. Even rabbis would scorn the
prospect of this child coming through God's open
door to pray—and offered Galilee a place in heaven
if only he would keep his distance:

> out of place,
> out of the place of worship.

All this was

> spiritually damaging,
> emotionally damaging,
> psychologically damaging, and
> physically damaging

to Galilee, so much so that eventually the youth became deaf. Years went by and Galilee was no longer
a youngster; he was a full-grown adult. But some
people treated Galilee as if he had never grown an
inch. Galilee was an outcast in the true meaning of
that word.

The word spread that Jesus was going by the
marketplace on his way to the synagogue, where he
was expected to preach. This was the synagogue
Galilee wasn't welcomed at, mind you.

A few of Galilee's friends

> begged,
> pleaded, and finally
> persuaded

Galilee to seek Jesus out and ask for his mercy.

Galilee approached Jesus and rather nervously and in a monotone voice, said, "S-s-sir w-w-will y-you-ou c-c-cu-cu-cure m-m-m-me?"

Jesus took Galilee's hand and told him to follow him to the synagogue. When they arrived at the synagogue, no one dared question them. The leaders of the synagogue recognized the authority of Jesus and stepped aside. When it was time to read the scroll, Jesus asked Galilee to read. Totally unprepared, but filled with faith, Galilee mounted the reading stand and read from the book of the prophet Isaiah:

> The spirit of the Lord is upon me,
>   because the Lord has anointed me;
> He has sent me to bring glad tidings
>   to the lowly, to heal the broken-hearted...

Those who knew of Galilee's life struggle were left joyfully spellbound while those who held Galilee in contempt were left dumbfounded because they could only recall how Galilee used to be. These same people, who had belittled Galilee, heard from his mouth a strong, firm voice proclaiming justice; heard
>   excellent pronunciation,
>   superb articulation, and
>   superior elocution.

Galilee, knowing the spirit of the Lord was upon him, departed, never to stutter or stammer again!

■ *"Love your enemies"*

7th Sunday in Ordinary Time (A)   *Matthew 5:38-48*

But I say to you, love your enemies, and pray for
  those who persecute you...

There was a time when I read this passage feeling
somewhat guilty because I never took it seriously. I
was seldom, if ever, challenged by it. The reason I
suppose I never took this scripture passage too
seriously was because it challenged me to
>   rehash old stuff,
>   replay old tapes,
>   return to old hurts.
It gave me the opportunity to brood once again.

If the truth be known, there is a need in me to brood
over wounds I have, caused by people in the past
who probably even to this day hold grudges against
me.

In pondering old wounds, I can vividly recall the actions done to me by my "enemies," though I thought
they were all forgotten. In a sense, when I con-

veniently ignore the challenge in this passage, I am off the hook; I am held to no accountability.

My adrenalin perks as I go through the litany of people—even back to my childhood—and replay all the thoughts, words, and deeds done me unjustly. I bristle as I brood.

There was Sammy, who pushed me off the monkey bars in the playground, laughing with the other children as I lay with blood coming from my head.

There was Joey from my old high school, whom I picked a fight with, he a freshman and I a senior. He beat me unmercifully, tarnishing my tough-guy image with ridicule that lasted for months.

And then there was Murph, my foreman at the factory, who accused me of being lazy and suspended me ten days. I pleaded my innocence but to no avail. For a while thereafter, the company was suspicious of me and my production.

And Sally, my college English professor, who insulted me to no end when she told the class my composition had no relationship with good English.

And Sharon, a sweetheart of sorts, who told me I was only a child and silly when I told her I cared for her very much. Tears have welled up in my eyes many times since; and even today, I think what a horrible thing to say to someone who has something very nice to say to someone else.

Even into my forties, I'm finding fault with people and will remember whatever hurts come from relationships. Of all the "forgotten" hurts that this passage rekindles in my mind, the "abandonment" of me by my natural parents ranks first. I carried

        that hurt,

        that resentment

on my back, a boulder weighing me down. For so many years I felt I was

        the cause,

        the problem,

        the burden;

felt I had done something wrong; felt my natural parents disowned me because I did not fit the bill of what a child ought to be like.

I brooded: Were my natural parents being caring or just plain callous?

Was it

        the lack of money,

        family trouble,

        peer pressure?

Was it

        the loss of a job,

        an already crowded house?

Might it have been a public scandal? Perhaps drugs? Was it loose living?

Could it have been for my own best interest: Did they live in a rat-infested house in the ghetto? Possibly a house so full of tension that even the walls and partitions reverberated?

Maybe someone was an abuser of children and I was given up for my own protection?

Whatever it may have been, living with the knowledge that my natural parents gave me up—and not knowing the *why*—was a tremendous hurt and the cause for a great amount of anger I expressed toward others.

In my mind, my natural parents were indeed my enemies; other "enemies" just happen to represent them.

But when it comes down to it, my anger and frustration was really aimed at the One who could have alleviated all the pain in my life. More than anyone, God, the Creator, could have intervened in my life,
> could have foreseen all that was to
> > happen,
> could have stopped it all,
> could have yelled "Enough!"

But God never did! But neither did God intervene when his Son was on the cross.

God created the very people who created a lot of hurt and pain for me. Yet I was taught that same God loves me! It never made sense to me—a complete contradiction, if you will.

When I add 2 + 2, I get 4, and when I add 4 + 4, I get 8, so and so forth. That makes for a lot of sense. But when I added love and hurt, I seldom, if ever, saw God. Instead I saw God as the enemy as well. After all, that seemed very logical to me.

Gradually, after many soul-searching years and in-
numerable difficult situations, I've grown to have a
better grasp of what it means to forgive and forget.
And it happened, somehow, that I reconciled my
anger with God. I then realized love and hurt can
equal love, can equal God!

Today I feel better about myself, and that feels good.
And today I am truly able to forgive
>   God,
>   my natural parents,
>   all the others, and most especially,
>   *myself!*

■ *Samaritan Woman*

3rd Sunday in Lent (A)   *John 4:5-42*

The middle-aged Samaritan woman, whose name was Sarah, knew someday the right man would come her way. She had been waiting a long time—and time, as we know, can be cruel. But Sarah would know that right moment; she knew happiness would come her way.

Sarah's mother told her after the fifth unsuccessful marriage that she should take a look at herself and accept who she was and be happy.

Then one day Sarah was approaching the well at Sheckem. The well was at the center of town, and it is where people gathered to talk things over, a sort of meeting place. The well had served the needs of this Samaritan town for centuries. The water not only quenched the thirst of weary travelers and villagers seeking respite, it also was used for washing cloths and dirt and grime from the faces of these hard-working people.

One day a traveler from Galilee came and rested his weary bones near the well; several companions were with him. Realizing it would be well to rest for a couple days, the traveler sent his companions to town to get sorely needed supplies.

A short time later, Sarah approached the well. She was balancing a yoke on her shoulders, which carried two buckets, one on each end, to be filled with the day's water. As Sarah neared the well, but still some distance away, she could make out the figure of the man. Having gone through this so many times in the past, she thought it was one of her former husbands—but which one?

"Is it Reuben?" Sarah said to herself, "The one who always insulted me in front of others? The one who abused me? If so, should I drop everything and head back home? No, it's not him," Sarah sighed with relief.

Walking ever so slowly now, Sarah thought it might well be another former husband, Benjamin. "If it is Benjamin," she mumbled to herself, "he may well expect the $3,500 I owed him after he caught me stealing from his business after the separation." Sarah quickly thought, "I don't have it to give back. Should I just turn back and pretend I really didn't need water today so as not to meet him?" A silent *no* came forward.

Continuing toward the well, the human silhouette still before her, Sarah yelled faintly, "Samuel! Samuel!?" But it wasn't Samuel, the one spouse she truly loved and continued to care for.

"Nathan? Could it be Nathan?" That marriage failed because commitment was part of a facade for both. "If it is, I'll just ignore him completely and continue my work," reasoned Sarah.

Now Sarah, about twenty feet away, realized it wasn't Nathan. But could it be her most recent husband, Aaron? Aaron had been
> the most promising,
> the most successful

of all her husbands. He was a diplomat. "It was," Sarah reflected, "because Aaron was so successful that our marriage failed." Consequently, Aaron lost his post and reputation.

Reaching the well, Sarah realized that the silhouette she was seeing was a traveler whom she knew not. But the traveler seemed to know her, and this confused Sarah. After some small talk, the traveler asked Sarah for water. "Get the water yourself! Look at you, a Jew asking for water! You've never had any trouble taking our water in the past—so why all of sudden are you asking help of me, a woman, and worse yet, a Samaritan?"

Taken back by surprise, the traveler pleaded ignorance and offered to help the woman with her water. She responded, "I do well by myself, sir." The traveler's remark, "You really don't," halted the woman in midstream. Looking back at him, she asked what he meant. "What I meant is what I see in your face," the traveler retorted. The woman, whose curiosity now heightened, put the buckets down and asked the traveler to explain.

He immediately put his hands into her buckets and brought forth water and said, "Your water indeed gives you life, but a life of broken promises and failed attempts to find happiness; a life of trial and error, as are the lives of people you have come in contact with." A bit shocked at the insight of the traveler, the woman queried him to explain further. "It's the way you look, your face. I see the strains of your life in the lines of your face; I know your help-lessness and your failures." With hesitation, she asked the traveler if he was a prophet, for she had never heard someone speak with such insight and knowledge. The traveler then placed one of the buck-ets in the sun and asked the woman to look in and take a look at her reflection. The woman did as he asked. He then asked her to tell him what she was seeing.

The woman told the traveler that she saw a broken, fragile person. "I see," she continued,

> my sadness,
> my lack of trust,
> my abrasiveness,
> my despair.

But, wait! I see more!

> I see goodness in me,
> I see the ability to overcome,
> I see sensitivity and love in me,
> I see a better me,
> I see a wonderful creation, a new
>   creation.

The woman looked at the traveler and, after a long pause, said, "You are a prophet, sir."

■ *"Is it lawful to pay...tax to Caesar...?"*

29th Sunday in Ordinary Time (A)   *Matthew 22:15-22*

> Then repay to Caesar what belongs to Ceasar and to God what belongs to God (Matthew 22:21).

There are only a few words that can instantly strike fear and terror in the hearts of people.

> Flood.
> Blizzard.
> Tornado.
> Hurricane.
> Earthquake.

These are natural disasters that send people fleeing for their lives. Just the mere mention of such words has people thinking about protecting their property and wondering how the cleanup operation will be handled if the mention of devastation becomes reality.

No word nor weather, however, can destroy anyone quite like the word "Rumor." Rumor has a life of its own; Rumor can send panic through the very lives of people and town alike—and destroy reputations.

We hear Rumor all around us:

> "She's been sleeping with you know
> who."
> "You know, he's gay. Look at the way
> he walks, the way he talks."
> "Did you hear he's going to a shrink?"
> "Haven't you heard she had an
> abortion?"

And how do we respond? Do we preserve the life of Rumor?

When the Pharisees sent their disciples to question Jesus about paying census tax to Caesar, what do you suppose would have happened if the Master had taken the one side over the other? Rumor! Rumor would have circulated around the entire town that Jesus was defying the authority of Caesar, or defying the authority of God. Whatever the case, Jesus would have had his hands full trying to explain what he meant.

Jesus defused the would-be Rumor by using common sense and cleverness, for he knew what was being planned and plotted, and he responded in kind. And Rumor died before it got started.

Ironically, it was Rumor that Jesus called God his Father and Daddy that ultimately led to his death.

Today, Rumor is still destroying.

Just last month Rumor caused a city-wide panic in which the reputations of many people were left in ruin. In a well-known metropolitan city stood a store—the most famous footlong hot dog store in the country. Doggie's, as it was called, had been a landmark for fifty years or more. Tourists from far and wide joined the local folks in acclaiming the tastiness of Doggie's product. Selling 3,000 footlong hot dogs a day wasn't out of the ordinary for such a legendary place striving to satisfy the appetites of so many. But in a matter of weeks, Doggie's business dropped eighty percent. The famous hot dog shop was selling only six-hundred footers a day. All because of a rumor that someone who worked at Doggie's had contracted elephantiasis, a disease that effects the bones in a way that causes abnormal growth. Though elephantiasis is not contagious, Rumor spread like wildfire in the thick forest of people's misconception.

Not only did Rumor go around town that someone had elephantiasis, but now, that someone had died from the disease! Rumor mushroomed. Business died in an instant. People started talking to one another,
> over the telephone,
> over the radio,
> over the television.

Like a bus out of control heading toward downtown shoppers, nothing could stop Rumor.

People began demanding proof from the employees working at Doggie's to ensure they were not stained with the disease. Away from Doggie's, the employees were being harassed when they went to restaurants and movie theaters. Even at sporting events, people shouted obscenities at the employees.

Rumor peaked last week, and Doggie's had to lay off ten workers. As a way of combating Rumor, the remaining four employees consented to be tested for elephantiasis.

But the damage had been done.

How did Rumor get started? It is believed that one of the employees had a heart attack a few months ago. But does that matter? Rumor took on a life of its own, as Rumor often does. And there are always people, even intelligent people, who are determined to believe the most preposterous story.

It's bad enough that elephantiasis eventually kills its victims. Now Rumor was killing reputations and businesses as well. Common sense was the first to die.

The power of Rumor is so strong that we have little, if any, control over it. The Son of God knew he could not stop the uncontrollable power of Rumor. If not him, how us?

■ *Transfiguration of Jesus*

2nd Sunday in Lent (A)   *Matthew 17:1-9*

Peter, James, and John were the ones who could tes-
tify to the Transfiguration. But this phenomenon
was in actuality the disciples'
> own trasfiguration,
> their own self-understanding:
> insight,
> knowledge,
> wisdom.

They saw Jesus as Jesus truly was. Their new understanding ensured that
> the message,
> the Master's life, and
> the promise
would be seen in a brighter light. Because of that
event on that mountain, the disciples' undertaking
became clearer.

We ourselves, like the disciples, are on a journey to
the mountain that will give us understanding; where
> insight,

knowledge, and
wisdom
will transform us and the world around us. But the
first step, the hardest, is to
see ourselves,
look inside ourselves, and
know ourselves.
In that way transformation can be truly experienced.

It is always easier to see, to look, and to know someone else rather than taking a peek at ourselves. But
we don't feel comfortable doing that. We instinctively know when someone hasn't had enough sleep, or
when someone's been drinking, or even lying. But
can we look and see ourselves in the same manner?
Do we try? The season of Lent may be a good time to
truly search our hearts to find our true selves.

Sometimes to know the self is an eye-opening experience. Perhaps a story about a man, a husband
and father, may help. This person had a lot going for
him. In many ways, he had it made. He had
a wife,
four beautiful daughters,
a mortgage-free home,
a good, secure job,
a decent salary.

But his house was not a happy home. It was a house
that knew abuse; a house where fighting was an
everyday occurrence. It was a house where
insults,
ridicule,

> manipulation,
> intimidation, and
> threats

were commonplace. In this house, only one person deemed respect, and that was he. Then one day, the father's eldest daughter was killed in an auto accident. The death caught the family in a web of shock and grief. It also brought a family, often divided, together for one another—except the father.

While everyone mourned their loss, the father could only mourn for himself; he lost a daughter he hardly knew. He searched for memories, but they just weren't there. Though the rest of his family rallied around each other, the father wanted to be left alone. First, melancholy set in, and, shortly thereafter, a deep depression controlled him.

As a newly ordained priest and family friend, I was asked to come to speak and spend time with him; which I gladly did.

What the father was grappling with was the image of himself. He, for the first time,

> took a deep look at himself,
> saw exactly what kind of person he
>   was, and
> didn't want to know himself anymore.

I said to him, "You will have other chances. Look! One of your other daughters is about to give birth to your first granchild. You can give to that new child something you hadn't been able to give your own. You'll have another chance—and many more as time goes on."

That was several years ago.

Just last week I came into the man's town and stopped by the house to see him. There before
>
> my eyes,
> my very eyes,

I saw this once-despondent father playing with his three grandchildren on the living room floor! Never had I seen a happier person! Once they were tired from all their activity, they were all ushered out to the father's, rather *grandfather's*, car so that they could get some burger and fries!

The father shared with me later that he was grateful for his retirement years and a chance to share
>
> time,
> joy, and
> love

with his grandchildren.We can avoid some of these traps in life if we take the time to look at ourselves,
>
> closely,
> clearly,
> honestly,

before we're forced to do so; but even in adversity we can learn and grow as this father did.

■ *Drama of the Prodigal Son*

24th Sunday in Ordinary Time   *Luke 15:11-32*

(There is another part to the story of the prodigal son; it deals with both sons after the dust settles over the incident and both of them are again working at the father's estate.)

The two sons are feeding the horses at the stables.

ELDER SON: I want you to know that I hate you very much. You have not only taken Dad for a ride but me as well.

YOUNGER SON: Dad has forgiven me. Can't you?

ELDER SON: Dad has always loved you more than me. After all, you are the baby of the family. Dad was wrong to forgive you without an apology from you first. I was stuck here to do your share of the work *and* my work at the same time. You never had to do double work.

YOUNGER SON: I never wanted you to do my share of the work. I am sorry.

ELDER SON: Humph!

YOUNGER SON: Ever since I've known you, you seemed very unhappy; gloomy, as a matter fact. I have heard nothing but complaints from you. I don't think you've ever been satisfied with me or with anything. You seem to have a lot of anger toward me. What have I done to deserve it? Dad rejoiced when I chose to come home—why can't you? Can you not share a laugh or even a smile with me?

ELDER SON: Sure, I'm angry! And no wonder. When you were small, I wasn't allowed out with my friends because I had to babysit you when Dad went out. When feastdays came, or birthdays, or any family gatherings, you always got more than your share of attention. No one missed or noticed me. I used to get so upset.

YOUNGER SON: I never knew I was getting all the attention. I can see why you would be unhappy. Have you ever mentioned this to Dad?

ELDER SON: No, I didn't think it would do any good. I thought he wouldn't listen to me.

YOUNGER SON: Dad loves you; he would have listened if you had only tried. Incidentally, you never told me how you felt toward me. If you had, it would have made our living together more productive in the long run. It would have said you cared about our relationship.

ELDER SON: You wouldn't have understood if I had told you; you were too young.

YOUNGER SON: Not too young to feel hurt or see anger in your eyes. I felt hurt many times when I sensed you hated me.

ELDER SON: It's not that I hated you; but you got all the toys when we were younger, while I received nothing.

YOUNGER SON: Yes, I did. But that wasn't because Dad loved me any more than you; it was because the family business grew and Dad could finally afford toys. By that time, you were too old for toys!

ELDER SON: But Dad lavished you with trips and outings, while I was left alone.

YOUNGER SON: Dad loves you very much. You were always dressed in the best clothes. Do you remember all the holiday outfits you wore? You looked great! All I wore were your hand-me-downs. But I never hated you. I felt happy for you.

ELDER SON: Dad always defended you when you and I fought.

YOUNGER SON: He did, but Dad was the teacher during those times. We both learned that fighting was wrong. But I never stopped loving you when you picked on me in front of your friends; when I wasn't allowed to play baseball with you and your gang; and even when my nose was bloody, I wanted you to be my brother more than anyone else in the world.

ELDER SON: You did?

YOUNGER SON: Yeah.

ELDER SON: Why?

YOUNGER SON: Because family is more important than a fight or two; love is more important than hate; brothers are more important than the things that make us different.

ELDER SON: But Dad always hugged you.

YOUNGER SON: Dad was hugging you too, but your eyes were closed and your mind was on those things that disturbed you and your vision.

ELDER SON: So Dad loves me?

YOUNGER SON: Yes. And so do I.

The two brothers hug each other with love and forgiveness!

■ *Baptism of the Lord*

1st Sunday in Ordinary Time (C)   *Luke 3:15-22*

Water. Water is crucial to our very existence. Without water, we couldn't be.

We can be without a lot and still be; we cannot be without water and still be.

> Without money, we can simply be;
> Without food, we can barely be;
> Without water, we cannot be.

It was food that destroyed humanity's first couple; it was money that destroyed humanity's greatest betrayer; and it was water that destroyed all living creatures, save two of each, in Noah's time. But, it was water that saved God's chosen people as they began

> their exile,
> their searching,
> their journey to the promised land.

Journey.

Journey is essential to our very existence; in fact, journey is the movement of our existence. Without journey, we couldn't be.

We can be without a lot and still be; we cannot be without journey and still be.

> Without purpose, we can simply be;
> Without desire, we can barely be;
> Without journey, we cannot be.

It was desire that set Joseph's brothers into a frenzy; and it was purpose that destroyed Cain. It was Jonah's fearful journey from God's command that resulted in his being swallowed by a whale. But, it was journey in the desert that saved all God's people.

Water and journey seem to go hand in hand in God's mysterious, magnificent plan of creation.

Noah's journey of a new age began as the flood waters receded; Moses was fetched from the Nile, and he was destined to begin the journey of a new era as he passed through the Red Sea.

And Jesus began
> his journey,
> his mission,
> God's new Covenant from the waters
> of the Jordan.

Jesus humbly walked into the
> still,
> stale,
> dead

waters of the Jordan, and when he emerged, the waters seemed to have been rejuvenated: its dullness gave way to

> sparkling,
> beaming,
> shining

life, as if to foretell the mission of the Master to those gathered.

Many of us (if not all of us) have begun our journey in the water of baptism. Each of us has inherited a piece of history.

Each of us,

> by water and
> by journey,

has accepted the mission Jesus gives us:

> "Love God and your neighbor as
>   yourself."
> "Love one another as I have loved
>   you."
> "Love your enemy."
> "Do not judge unless you are willing
>   to be judged."
> "Forgive not seven times, but 70 x 7
>   times."

The Jordan was only the first of Jesus' experiences of journeying with water:

> He changed water to wine;
> He gave water to a Samaritan;
> He calmed the waters of the sea;
> He cured the blind man at the pool;
> He told whale stories about Jonah
>   while on the river;

He went fishing at a nearby lake;
He clowned with Peter by walking on
    water; and then,
He got serious and washed his
disciples' feet.

We too can do a lot with water:
    We can water our vegetable garden
      and give what we grow to the poor;
    We can give water to a passerby;
    We can wipe tears from our
      neighbor's eyes;
    We can wash a wound;
    We can cook;
    We can change;
    We can cure.

Jesus' journey from the Jordan ended in Jerusalem—and death; our journey from baptism will also end in death.

Jesus' death was a journey to life—lasting life; our death will also be a journey to life—everlasting life!

■ The Pharisee and the Sinner

30th Sunday in Ordinary Time (C)   *Luke 18:9-14*

There was once a well-known, world-renowned dignitary who came to the White House for a long-awaited visit. Just as the dignitary stepped out of the chartered Concord non-stop flight from Paris, he received a tumultuous round of applause that made all present proud to be in his company, including the President of the United States.

The chief executive invited the honored guest to join him for a hearty dinner and a leisurely chat afterward.

At dinner's conclusion, the two men went to the President's private living quarters so they could have a casual talk without any interruption. In the background, a voice barely audible came from the television set as both parties settled down for a relaxing chat.

The President began the conversation: "Well, what have you been up to since the last time we met?"

"I've been very busy of late, Mr. President. I just pledged $100,000 for a drug rehabilitation program in Chicago. I don't know what to think; the whole country's gone to pot, drugs you know. My pledge is the least I can do. Oh sure, I'll take another scotch, on the rocks, please. My favorite, Chivas Regal; wouldn't touch anything else."

The television newscaster's voice came softly from across the room. "Actress Elizabeth Taylor left the Betty Ford Center in good spirits after being hospitalized for drug and alcohol dependency..."

The President's guest continued. "The Northern Ireland problem? That's another lost cause. You know as well as I do that religious war will never end. Neither the Catholics nor the Protestants are anxious for peace; all they want is to destroy each other. The best policy is to ignore the both of them. I am glad my faith is not involved in such preposterous causes and emotions. I mind my own business, Mr. President, and say my prayers."

The sounds from the television floated around them. "The heads of the Roman Catholic Church and the Lutheran Church met today in West Germany. They both asked forgiveness from one another."

"And the same with the Middle East conflict," the guest went on. "It's impossible to bring any good to that part of the world. I should know, I've been there and I have studied the problem. The only good policy is to continue sending arms and supplies. You know what they say about the Jews and the Arabs, Mr. President, don't you? They'll fight forever—and I say let them fight each other to submission; and that's to our advantage."

The reporter's voice gently sounded, "Recapitulating today's historic events: Anwar el-Sadat, the leader of Egypt, and Menachim Begin, the leader of Israel, signed a treaty at Camp David banning war between their two countries. This signifies genuine hope for a world eager for peace."

"Me, enter politics?" asked the President's visitor. It's of no interest to me. I'm not attracted to the mudslinging that goes on. It seems to me that everyone is out for themselves at other people's expense. I'm not like that; I pride myself to a better standard than that. When have you ever heard a politician take ownership of wrongs done in the name of politics, Mr. President?"

"Today's top story:" the newscast continued. "It is reported that Hubert H. Humphrey, in his final days, has contacted those whom he may have offended in the heat of political battle and asked forgiveness."

"My children? I'm glad you asked, Mr. President," the guest smiled. "Jimmy is fine; he's in graduate school. My eldest daughter has graduated from nursing school and is working at the community hospital. I have three others in high school. Donna, the middle child, who just graduated from high school, is giving her mother and me fits. We told her to mind our rules or leave the house. Well, she left, and now she's tasting the real world. These kids today, you can't tell them anything. You know as well as I, we live in a permissive society where anything goes—and the AIDS epidemic? It's disgusting. If my kids were to ever— My God, I'd break every bone in their bodies. Sex, it's too easy today; and all this pre-marital nonsense, and homosexuality. Well, I'm doing my share. Besides my personal $50,000 check, my foundation has set up a special fund to combat the filth on our streets—and we need your country's support, Mr. President. Oh, by the way, I've started divorce proceedings; that's how hectic my life's been. Chocolate Mousse pie!? Sounds terrific!"

As the two world leaders began eating their dessert, the news reporter read the latest. "A New York City study issued today estimated that up to two million juvenile runaways come to the city yearly. Nearly eighty percent are engaged in prostitution. The study lauded the work of Covenant House, a shelter for runaways, whose emphasis is caring, feeding, and counseling youth displaced by home and environment."

■ *"...in the breaking of bread."*

Once upon a time, there were two boys who were the best of buddies—they were inseparable. Their names were Larry and Kenny. They only lived a block or two from each other and had known each other as far back as they could remember. They were at the age now that girls sparked their attention—and grades only somewhat.

Speaking of grades, even though Kenny was several months younger than Larry, he was the smarter and wiser of the two. This frustrated Larry, especially when he had to "go to war" just to maintain a C average. Kenny, without really trying, most always received A's. Many of their friends looked up to the younger of the twosome; several of the students at the high school sought assistance from Kenny, who gave it willingly. Even Larry's parents looked at Kenny's leadership in trying to better understand the younger generation. This did not sit well with Larry.

Larry, however, managed to keep his frustrations under control; he never grew too despondent and kept his feelings hidden deep inside himself. Larry valued his relationship with Kenny too much to make a fuss of it all. But, finally, after their high school graduation ceremony, a rupture occurred in the friends' relationship. At the family celebration, Kenny, who was valedictorian of their class, spent the entire time with family, friends, and other students. It seemed everyone wanted to be associated with the "brightest".

Everyone seemed to forget about Larry—after all, he just barely made it. It had been understood that Kenny and Larry would have a combined celebration, but that part was forgotten in all the fuss over Kenny.

Time went on, and Kenny became a law student. He and Larry, who worked at his uncle's bakery, communicated less frequently. This strained their relationship to the point of non-existence.

Upon completion of law school and passing the state bar exam, Kenny joined a prestigious law firm in their hometown. This excited Kenny—and nearly everyone else. The leaders of the community and many other people of influence received the new attorney with much pleasure and fanfare. Larry, in the meantime, continued working at the bakery. Though he wished for a better lot, Larry never really felt out of place in his position nor jealous of his friend, who was getting to be one of the more recognized people of the community.

Larry did, however, wish Kenny would take their relationship more seriously. He sensed the relationship was not like it once was, ever since that high school graduation party. It further seemed to Larry that whenever he and Kenny got together, which wasn't too often, he felt a sense of competition from Kenny—or worse yet, a putdown of Larry's lot in life. Kenny would argue that what really counted in life were

> brains,
> looks,
> position,
> money,
> power,
> influence,
> dress,
> sex.

"If you were to use your full ability, you would be more than a breadmaker," Kenny criticized. Larry for his part offered little, if any, rebuff, somehow knowing that things would eventually correct themselves.

Professionally, Kenny did quite well. He established himself in a niche that brought him megabucks and never quarreled over all the attention. Corporations sought Kenny out. Many times, various corporate leaders would woo Kenny with the finest foods in the most plush restaurants in the most exclusive part of town, trying to garner his expertise. Kenny had an enormous appetite—loved all kinds of food, especially sandwiches.

In the meantime, Larry's uncle died, leaving his much-loved nephew the bakery for all his years of service to him and his business. Having the bakery was a godsend, Larry would often say. With a broad smile, friendly persuasion, and a good product, Larry started selling his specially made bread to a whole new line of customers, including many of the more plush restaurants.

One day at the city's annual ethnic celebration, where various nationalities brought their sandwiches to sell, a debate took place as to which was the most important ingredient in the making of a great sandwich. Many said it was the meats; others said it was the seasonings; there were those who said it was the lettuce and tomato, while others said it was the mustard, ketchup, and mayonnaise. Still others said it was the bread. With no consensus, the crowd called on the expert for a definitive decision. They called on Kenny.

When Kenny came over to settle the dispute, he tasted several of the sandwiches they had there and declared that it was

> the meats,
> the seasonings,
> the lettuce and tomato, and
> the mustard, ketchup, and
> mayonnaise

that made a sandwich a sandwich! About the same time, Larry drove his truck to the site to unload his bread and rolls. Though Larry and Kenny nodded at one another, nothing indicated the steadfast relationship that once had been. Over the years that relationship had deteriorated to just a nod. Once Larry finished unloading, Kenny, always the center of attention, belittled his former friend's occupation saying, "Breadmaking is not a suitable occupation these days." The crowd seemed to enjoy—even laughed at—this insult at Larry's expense.

Some months later, there was a reception at the city's convention center to celebrate the Man of the Year. Sitting on the dais were the mayor, city council president, and many of the city's best and finest. They were there to laud the accomplishments of Kenny, who was indeed the Man of the Year. One by one, each of the dignitaries told of the deeds that this young man had given done for his community, and how grateful the community was. One dignitary who spoke Kenny's praises was his parish priest.

Kenny's pastor extolled him for his service to others and suggested that the bread Kenny received at weekly communion allowed for his service to others.

Later that night, after being bestowed with honors never before imagined, Kenny took a ride in his car alone to view "his" city, which he loved. Driving past his church, Kenny noticed Larry leaving his freshly baked bread at the church door for consumption at tomorrow's service.

Kenny realized his failure to his friend. In the breaking of the bread the next day, Kenny saw the wholeness in Larry—and in renewed friendship.

■ *"For God so loved the world..."*

4th Sunday in Lent (B)   *John 3:14-21*

When I was about nine years old, I often gazed in
wonder at the glorious sights all around me. Most
especially, I admired the trees that lined the
boulevard for miles and miles. It was the leaves on
the trees that fascinated me and my imagination.
Autumn was the best and most obvious time for me
to think creatively.

Autumn leaves are a spectacle to behold, when all
the world's colors assimilate, making a great garden
of nature.

> The crisp orange,
> the mellow yellow,
> the blushing red,
> the shy pink,
> the fading green,
> the bold brown

made me want to know God even more. I feel if God
can give leaves such marvelous colors, surely God
can make me—and everyone—just as beautiful.

But when my thoughts leveled off, and autumn gave way to winter, I again wondered a child's thought: "What happens to all the leaves landscaping the trees?"

There comes a time, I observed, when leaves become
> boring,
> tired, and
> old.

The irritable winds have left the leaves mangled in disarray, hopelessly
> battered,
> bruised, and
> limp.

The leaves, their colors now a scorched amber, swished by the wind's finale, are loosened from their branches and begin their descent to the earth. They
> flutter,
> float,
> fall with all the grace Mother Nature
> can offer, distracted occasionally by
> an acorn thumping to the ground.
> The leaves lay on the ground, the
> burial place for the fallen crackly
> skeletons that once had life.

Everywhere I walked, piles of dead leaves were visible. The fallen leaves began to rot, and all the more when the neighborhood children came to play after school, trampling the leaves into a thousand particles.

In those days, my chore to earn spending money from my parents was to rake our lawn and pile the dead leaves in brown shopping bags for the trash collectors to pick up. No sooner did the trash collectors take our bundles of leaves than did the whole process seem useless. By nightfall, leaves by the multitudes were once again scattered all over the lawn.

What fascinates me now about this whole process is the connection all this has with people: their birth, their falling from grace that we call sin, and their redemption.

You see, the beauty of this life cycle began some time ago when, as buds, leaves seemed to appear out of nowhere to burst forth into an everglowing green. With the change of season, the leaves turn to brilliant hues that leave humanity in awe. No sooner do we see this brilliance than it is time for the leaves to fall to earth. The end, as we perceive, is when the trash collectors come to pick up the leaves for their final proper burial: the incinerator. The leaves that remain? They are doomed to seep into the soil forever.

The leaves that once exhibited unreal beauty are now rotted into the soil. Ironically, those leaves, in due time, become the soil that spurs new life: soil that gives life to earth's inhabitants.

People go through a similar process; we call it reconciliation. The process begins at birth, and as people come into their own,
> their own individual beauty shines;
> their character takes shape;

71

> their gifts and talents blossom;
> their goodness irradiates

the entire world. But as good intentions become mired in self-serving attitudes, people

> begin to fall,
> begin to hurt

others, which causes fallen hearts and minds. The brilliance of people

> fades;
> falls *Thump!*

and they all lie facedown in shame.

However, as with the leaves that fall, God has a purpose for fallen people.

> It is in the falling,
> it is in the utter collapse,

that people,

> in all their frailty,
> with all their weaknesses, indeed,
> with all their sins

have the ability to heal others and to heal themselves as when they were

> good,
> beautiful,
> strong, and
> unfallen.

People have the power to continue life, though fallen, because Jesus said the power of God willed it so—because the power of God's love is healing.

■ *The Prodigal Son Parable (I)*

24th Sunday in Ordinary Time (C)   *Luke 15:11-24*

"Large pepperoni pizza, please!"

Except for Thanksgiving dinner with all the trimmings, pizza is by far my favorite meal.

In the major industrial city that I come from, the area population of which numbered some four million, there were as many pizza places as there were churches.

Moving, however, to a small town of five thousand, there are only two pizza places to chose from. And that presents certain problems/dilemmas for me.

The more well-known pizza establishment has the best-tasting pizza in town—but, God, it's so expensive! A pizza with pepperoni cost $4.50 more than the rival place across town. With my meager salary, it comes as no surprise that I frequent the less expensive pizza house. If sin is lusting for something, then I'm going to pay for it because I lust constantly for the more expensive pizza.

One night it happened. Driving home a few Monday nights ago, I had a pizza crisis—and the more expensive pizza place was right in front of me. I didn't care how much it was going to cost; all I knew was I had hunger pangs and saliva oozing from my mouth!

"Large pepperoni pizza, please," I ordered. "That'll be $8.10," the cashier said. With an uncertain smile I exclaimed, "Eight dollars?!" The cashier explained that Monday evenings were considered Family Night, thus reducing the regular charge.

Leaving the establishment quite satisfied, I programmed that information in my mind for future reference.

A couple weeks later, driving by the same establishment on a Monday evening, I decided to order a large pepperoni pizza. The same cashier with her monotone voice spoke: "That'll be $12.60." With a sudden jerk of my body and an obviously quizzical look on my face, I questioned, "Twelve dollars?" After replying in the affirmative, the cashier proceeded to inform me that the Family Special didn't begin till 5 P.M.—and it was only 4:52 P.M.

"That's only eight minutes!" I protested to no avail, especially when she reminded me that I placed my order twenty minutes before. To pay for the pizza, having only eight dollars with me, I had to go out to my car and grab all the change I store away for tolls, phone calls and emergencies—and this was such!

Driving on the interstate the following day, a trooper pulled me over for speeding. "How fast?" I asked.

"Sir, you were going two miles an hour above the limit," the officer responded.

"Two miles above the limit! Look at all the others!" I roared. Unmoved by my passion, the officer went about his business writing me a ticket.

I left the scene of this misdemeanor and, several miles up the interstate, soon approached the toll booth. I realized I was totally broke. No money, no change, no script, just nothing. The woman who was collecting the tolls rudely told me to pull to the edge of the highway and come inside to fill out an affidavit pledging to pay the state as soon as I returned home. "All this for twenty-five cents!?" I exclaimed. The tolltaker's only defense was to say that she worked for the state and was only doing her job.

Continuing my drive home, I could not help but think of my old high school English teacher, Sally Martischa. (Miss Martischa, no doubt, has by this time gone to her final and proper reward.) Having done miserably all year in her class with only a week and a half before the end of school (literally, since I was to graduate), Miss Martischa informed me that I would have to go to summer school if I should fail to achieve at least a sixty-five on my final English test.

Seldom had anything been said to me that made me as instant a nervous wreck as this incident. You see, my dad, in his great wisdom, had bribed me with his car. I wanted that car more than anything in the world at the time, so my dad and I had shaken hands on it. Now that I might not graduate, the car would never be mine!So you can understand the anxiety I was going through.

> I studied,
> and studied.
> Never did I study as hard.

On the next-to-the-last day, Miss Martischa returned the corrected test papers to all the students—except me. She told me to see her at the end of class. I felt somewhat proud. I really thought that I had done so well that Miss Martischa wanted to congratulate me in a special way for all my efforts.

But in the end, Miss Martischa handed me my paper with a sixty-four, saying that I had to repeat in summer school. I was

> shocked,
> bewildered.

All I could see was no car in my future.

Gasping for words, I said to Miss Martischa, "It's

> only a point!
> Only a point!
> A *point!*"

It made no difference. I was going to summer school, and the car would have to wait for another day.

In the parable of the prodigal son, the father who welcomes the son home is not like the pizza cashier who is held hostage to time, or the officer who is monitoring speed, or the tolltaker who collects money, or Sally Martischa who scores and grades—

no, that father is too ridiculous for all that. That father just wanted his son back!

Our God doesn't keep time, nor collect money, nor does God do anything else; God just loves us! Our God loves us in a totally ridiculous way—He is eagerly awaiting our return home!

(Read on for the sequel to this story.)

■ The Prodigal Son Parable (II)

24th Sunday in Ordinary Time (C)   *Luke 15:11-24*

In our parable story, the father comes out running toward the younger son to welcome him home after squandering his share of the estate. What a radical love—some would say ridiculous love—the father has for such an indiscrete son. While some might/should rejoice at this kind of love being displayed, others resent it.

There are an assortment of reasons why people will resent attention, care, and love that is shown to others. The reasons are many:

> jealousy,
> envy,
> selfishness,
> pride.

The elder son in our parable is such a person. From his perspective, he is absolutely right. And he represents, many times, us! The elder son is doing all the labor, "a slave," as he puts it while telling his father, "This son of yours has been running amok, doing everything under the sun while the chores at home have been left completely ignored. And you're going to celebrate his return while I've been working like a dog?!" All the angriness in seeing his father pamper his kid brother; all the bitterness of seeing his father lavish his kid brother with love was too much for him to take. He had to let his father know his feelings, and in doing so, he had to face feelings toward his sibling that he had not even acknowledged before.

What the elder son did was put his father in a "no win" situation; the father had to recant everything he said to the younger son or risk the loyalty of the elder son.

The father chose neither. His love
        was always there,
        is on-going,
        is ever-growing.

The elder son's tantrum is not unlike all of ours when given moments in our lives that don't "fit our bill." Many of us, if not all, can remember when, for one reason or another, we didn't like someone, and we
        expected, perhaps,
        demanded
our friends to feel likewise, even though their feelings may have been quite different. And if they failed to meet our expectations, they might have been in danger of losing our friendship.

That is precisely what the elder son wanted the father to do: to listen to him and obey his wishes.

I have a friend who had a falling out with a business partner because of poor and sloppy management. Whatever relationship that had developed from their association deteriorated when the separation occurred. The magnitude of the fallout became clear when both parties were taken to court to prove the bankruptcy they had claimed.

My friend lost everything as did his partner. Both had hostile feelings toward each other, each thinking the other had failed the business. They both stopped seeing each other, and their separation lasted for many years.

One partner, over time, managed to do well in another career endeavor. But my friend never recovered any semblance of a business career he longed to have. His failure seemed complete when his marriage came apart at the seams. He decided to take a vacation alone to think of its ramifications on him and his family.

On the way home, he decided to visit his younger brother, who lived in an inviting bachelor's pad. The brothers were excited to see each other, for they had a lot to catch up on, since they hadn't seen each other in several months.

As both brothers entered the kitchen, the younger brother introduced a visiting guest to his brother. Their eyes met; lo and behold, it was the older brother's former business partner! Tension from both partners clouded the kitchen. Not a word was spoken. The younger brother, confused and shaken, asked if they had known each other.

The younger brother's guest left rather nervously, leaving the room to the two brothers. Berating his brother, the incensed elder brother demanded that the house not be accessible to his former partner. The brother listened without comment and earnestly tried to understand the situation as it had shown itself. Eventually, the brothers' conversation focused on the family matters that had precipitated the visit in the first place.

The following day, the older brother visited his younger brother again, and a replay of the day before occurred—to the absolute astonishment of everyone. The ex-partner was again a guest! The younger brother, not giving an inch to his brother's ranting, took him aside and told him of the love he had for him; nonetheless, his friend was his friend and his brother was his brother, and love knows both. Coming to his senses, the older brother approached his former partner and shook hands as if to say, "Let bygones be bygones."

The reconciliation was a relief for all, but most importantly for the older brother. For he soon realized that love can only produce love, and that love inhibited is love lost to everyone.

The older brother, my friend, also realized that in regaining love lost years ago, he could now begin to know himself again and be better able to handle what lay before him.

■ *Parable of the Corrupt Judge*

29th Sunday in Ordinary Time (C)   *Luke 18:1-8*

"No! No! No!" I said aloud to myself after reading this parable of the corrupt judge. This parable didn't seem to apply to me because I could never remember when someone in need had shown up at my front door in the middle of the night (or in the middle of the day for that matter), ringing the door bell in search of assistance and had not received it immediately.

As I closed the Good Book, I heard a sound outside my front door; a screeching sound that was most unusual and very annoying. I paid little attention the the sound because the rain that was falling was coming down in buckets, and with the early morning wind ruffling the nearby trees and bushes, I assumed that peculiar sound was the havoc outside. A few minutes later, I heard that peculiar sound again as I was downing my Rice Krispies mixed in with my Wheaties. I paused as if to go investigate but nixed that idea, thinking it was my imagination playing games with me.

But even with the noise of the falling rain upon the roof, I heard the sound again—and again and again. With all that, I was still stubborn: I wasn't going to investigate that sound, no matter how unusual.

Pouring my coffee into my City of Philadelphia mug, a daily morning ritual, I again chose to ignore the sound. As minutes went by, however, the insistent sound continued. It was unavoidable; I had to investigate.

Opening my front door, lo and behold, what I found was the ugliest dog I have ever seen in my life. A sorry-looking dog indeed. The creature must have been sleeping when cuteness was handed out. At first glance I realized that the dog's teeth were totally outside its mouth! This was a small thing that didn't make for an endearing pet to keep. Though its left ear was perfectly normal, the right ear, well, there wasn't a right ear! And, oh my, those droopy eyes guaranteed a wandering existence. The dog had a heavy limp because one of its legs was smaller than the other; its paws were striking because they seemed worth enough for a small lion—but not a medium-size dog. And I think the dog knew it and felt ashamed!

Making matters worse, its nose seemed a bit crooked, and he seemed not to know this. If the dog had, it would have been more depressed. All in all, the dog didn't fit anywhere, but that didn't alter the fact that it was at my front door crying for help, er, mercy?

The dog was so awful looking that once my investigation was over, I closed the door with no intention of reopening it for the beast. But that
>unusual,
>screeching,
>peculiar,
>annoying,
>awful

sound continued through the morning. I ignored it regardless how distracting. But the screeching continued.

As afternoon approached, I tried all kinds of ways to ignore that sound. But whatever I did, or wherever I went, that sound followed me. It dawned on me that the sound resembled the cry of an abandoned baby, and that bothered me. However, it didn't bother me enough to rescue the dog.

But the cry began to take its toll; it was wearing me down. I tried going about my routine of working, slipping out the back door, which leads to the church proper. But the dog followed me there—indeed everywhere I went,
>the dog,
>the sound

followed me. I tried so hard not to look at the beast, even closing my eyes as I walked/worked.

Finally, I gave in. As ineffective as I was, my heart finally took over. I brought in the beast, er, dog. With a towel, I dried the dog and fed him. I even allowed the visitor to lick my face and repeatedly I shook its paws. While being hospitable I noticed a collar around the dog's neck. On the collar there was a family's name and address.

After notification, the family came over to pick up their "baby." The word "baby" was somewhat contagious because as they were leaving I mentioned to the family that they had a pretty baby. Without a moment's hesitation, they responded, "Of course!"

This story illustrates just what we don't do for others when they don't look like the way we feel they should. Unfortunately, no matter how persistent one might be, the way they look will determine how they will be treated.

Just the other day, I read an article in the newspaper where a now-famous model, who was involved in a perceived political scandal that brought down a presidential candidate, recently said to a university seminar on ethics as she donned buckteeth and glasses, "If I looked like this, how long do you think my picture would be in the press?"

■ Jesus Expels Satan

There was a jumbo jet—the Trans-World Airline charter flight 790 was landing at JFK Airport in New York. There were 348 tourists and a crew of twelve that filed out from this flight returning from the Holy Land.

Among the passengers was a man who left this plane completely unnoticed. This slim man wore a perfectly tailored navy blue suit, a white shirt, and a subdued burgundy-striped tie. Over one arm he carried an overcoat; in his other hand he carried his briefcase. When this man gave his passport to the customs official, the official's jaw dropped and a wide-eyed stare crossed his face. The customs official, very confused at this point, looked at this bearded fellow and said incredulously, "You can't be Jesus Christ! Can you?" The docile passenger said that indeed he was Jesus Christ.

Jesus hailed a taxi on this bitterly cold afternoon and headed from the airport to the rundown, decaying streets of Harlem. The word was out that Jesus was here to cast out demons, the way he had done two thousand years ago.

As Jesus neared one of those highrise, low-income apartment buildings, he noticed a black family bundled together near some old, broken down furniture. They noticed that it was Jesus, and called out to him: "Jesus of Nazareth, have pity on us." When Jesus inquired as to their plight, they responded by saying, "Our landlord has evicted us; he says we are worthless. Are we possessed, as in days of old?" Overcome with compassion and grief, Jesus took a bus uptown to Park Avenue, where he knocked on the landlord's door. The landlord opened his solid chrome door, and asked, "Who are you?" Christ replied, "I am Jesus. I'd like to know if you are meeting the needs of my people?" A swift reply came: "Get out of my sight, you troublemaker!"

Later Jesus was walking the streets of Manhattan when a girl who was stripped of her clothing came running from a bar. She was crying hysterically. Jesus took his overcoat and covered her up. She recognized who he was and admitted that she was not worthy of his care. "I lose myself in my loneliness and fear," she sighed. At that same moment, a crowd surrounded both Jesus and the girl. The leader of the pack yelled to the Jesus, "Whoever you are, mind your own business!" Jesus spoke up and said, "People are my business, and you are destroying my property." With anger bordering on hostility, one final warning from the crowd sprung forth:

"Scram, the both of you; you're nothing but troublemakers."

It was getting late, and Jesus decided to take the subway to the Bronx. While on the subway, Jesus saw the many weapons people carry for protection. At the train's last stop, Jesus noticed a young Puerto Rican man lying by the tracks, badly bleeding. In this person's hand was a newly purchased gun; several rounds had been fired. The young man, near death, sought Jesus' healing and forgiveness. Jesus blessed the man and forgave him—"But please, for God's sake, look at the harm that is done and don't do it again." With that, Jesus took the gun and a couple of knives that were lying beside the man and put them in his briefcase.

There was an all-night pawn shop nearby, and Jesus entered the front door, amid much security equipment and personnel. Jesus approached the owner, who was smoking a rather large and expensive cigar. As Jesus inquired as to why this owner would sell guns and knives so that people could hurt one another, the owner responded immediately and directly: "No one tells me what to do, buddy. Move on, you troublemaker!" Jesus waited for a better answer, and the owner willingly but harshly added, "It's a dog-eat-dog world out there, and I am going to make money any way I can. I offer people protection." The contemptuous owner offered a final comment, "The more weapons a guy has, the better off he'll be." And the smoke from his cigar rose in the air alongside his words.

Jesus arrived back at the airport for a flight to somewhere. Jesus was troubled. In the old days, he
thought,

> those unclean spirits,
> those demons,
> all those Satans

recognized me, knew who I was, and left all those
people. But things seem a bit different these days.
Jesus sadly concluded, "The people who did not
recognize *me* do not recognize Satan either."

■ Transfiguration of Jesus

2nd Sunday in Lent (A)   **Luke 9:28-36**

The Transfiguration of Jesus is an experience of phenomenal proportions, a supernatural mystery. Like all supernatural events, little can be deciphered from it. For that reason, the Transfiguration ought not be a subject under a microscope like a frog being dissected in order to understand why a frog is a frog.

The mystery of the Transfiguration ought to be inspiring simply because it is a mystery. Nonetheless, our appetite for comprehension is greater than our belief in supernatural.

The Transfiguration would best make sense if people understood their many life experiences and the mysteries that go along with them. Then the mysteries connected with Jesus, including the Transfiguration, would be easier to understand.

But still we try for explanation.

In the Transfiguration reading, Jesus takes Peter, John, and James to the top of a mountain. In sight of his closest companions, Jesus is transfigured. As never before,
> not in Galilee,
> not in Cana,
> not at Caesarea Philippi,
this Jesus appears different:
> a transformation,
> a transfiguration,
> a trans-something
takes place. His disciples are starry-eyed, confused, and baffled. They are in awe, speechless—except Peter, who seldom is ever speechless. Peter in his excitement exclaims: "You are truly God, Jesus! We'll erect three monuments: one for you, one for Moses, and one for Elijah. What excellent timing! How good for us to witness this great event! Where's the Polaroid?!"

Jesus in effect, tells his companions to simply enjoy the moment of mystery and keep the event to themselves, to savor it inwardly.

But Peter wants none of that, insisting, "Enjoy? We want to celebrate! *Celebrate!* We need to have a party; we need to tell everyone! Where's the nearest phone?"

Jesus cautions Peter and the others not to get over-anxious. He tells them again to keep this moment inside themselves for pondering later when they will feel lost and abandoned.

But really, who could enjoy that moment without prodding its mystery?

I wonder if what Peter, John, and James saw that day was actually their own fullness, the realization of who Jesus was? Perhaps
> their vision changed,
> their mission became clearer,

perhaps
> the haziness left their eyes?

Maybe it wasn't Jesus who was transfigured but *they* themselves? Perhaps they began to see themselves as never before. Perhaps they now saw Jesus as usual but from a different perspective because they themselves had acquired truth and right? Their excitement of who they were actually got the best of them—especially Peter.

Jesus has a way of doing that!

Jesus' love transfigures us, too, and gives us the power
> of transforming one another,
> to transform ourselves.

We learn through our life experiences that transformation/transfiguration has two sides to it: one of transforming and one of being transformed.

To illustrate, there was once a gentle and kind man who attended to everyone's needs. This man had a friend whose lifestyle left much to be desired. When the man heard his friend was dying, he hastened to his bedside. When the man arrived, he whispered a few words of love to his dying friend, hoping that in the few remaining hours his friend would reconcile himself to the Maker. The friend died hours later, and the man was confident reconciliation had taken place. The man also believed the power of transformation had taken place, and he believed he had a hand in it.

Several years later, after allowing that single transforming event to control his life (something that happens to proud people), that same man fell to picking and choosing people he considered worthy of his attention. Then one day a couple whom the man had dismissed as nobodies told him a story that taught him a valuable lesson.

The couple's youngest son was tragically killed in an automobile accident. The driver, the son's friend, was intoxicated and escaped unharmed. As the grieving family united for the burial, an older son was planning revenge for the "slaughter." The mother, a shy person who never raised a storm with anyone, stopped her son in midtrack. She was going to handle the situation as only a mother could.

The mother left her home and walked three blocks to the house of her dead son's friend. The son's friend answered the door and in complete shock timidly invited the mother inside. The mother told the youngster that she would not want him to live his life in guilt. She added that she needed to forgive him and offered a hug and kiss. The relieved friend accepted—and experienced the gift of forgiveness.

Upon hearing this story, the man realized the power of transformation a second time; this time however, he was transformed. Never would he judge anyone again.

■ *Jairus' Daughter and the Woman Hemorrhaging*

13th Sunday in Ordinary Time (B)   **Mark 5:21-43**

As Jesus was making his way through the noontime crowd of people all bundled up doing their last minute Christmas shopping on this exceptionally cold and windy December day, there lay in bed two critically ill people. One was Maria, a very young girl who lay in an irreversible coma. She had been this way for a couple years, and many of her friends and neighbors felt Maria would be better off dead than continue this life of darkness.

From his spacious suburban home, Dominic, a young State Department official and father of this young girl, came by bus to the densely populated, noisy downtown area to get a glimpse of Jesus and appeal to him to allow Maria to recover from her terrible ordeal. Dominic thought if he got close enough and spoke to Jesus himself, "How could he refuse the life of a young child?"

The other person who lay critically ill was Rachel. Rachel, an elderly woman, was a patient at Saint Francis Nursing Home, where she lay suffering from a painful cancer that infested her entire body. Rachel constantly bemoaned the fact that she was old and decrepit and wished she could be young again and free from pain and disease.

Rachel was well aware of the travels of Jesus and knew he was only a few blocks away—within walking distance. She had heard the excitement surrounding all his cures, and she believed if she could get close enough to touch him she would be made well again. Rachel's husband, Reuben, a man of almost eighty years, had given up hope of any cure, whether from Jesus or anyone else. But Rachel, a woman of determination and spunk despite her infirmity, rose from her bed and began to walk toward the crowded area where Jesus was healing.

As Dominic deboarded the Shoppers' Express, he thought to himself, "If only Maria could live to a ripe old age; if only she could be given the chance to live to the fullest, it would be the merriest of all Christmases."

A block away from Jesus, Rachel slowly turned the corner, and the wind gashed her pale and thin face. Rachel could already sense the power coming from Jesus, which only reinforced her strong faith.

Though they didn't realize it, Dominic and Rachel were both seeking the fullness of life.

The crowds were shouting, pushing, and shoving as they tried to get a better look at this holy man, the likes of whom they had never seen. As Dominic neared Jesus, a great hesitation came over him, for he began to feel unworthy. But suddenly, something hidden in the very depths of Dominic's heart and soul, a gush of faith, moved him to approach Jesus. Just as this was happening, Rachel was pushing her way into the crowd, scattering the holiday packages people were carrying. Rachel's pain was excruciating and prevented her from getting any closer to Jesus. She stretched out her hand hoping and believing it would brush Jesus' overcoat.

Dominic asked Jesus, "Would you come to my house and heal my daughter?" At the same time, Rachel's fingers touched the overcoat and she immediately felt his healing power. At the other end of town, Maria awoke from her sleep.

Jesus said to them both, "Know that burden, pain, and death will always be part of the world. I cannot cure the world. However, *you* can if sin is cured in your lives. But for the short time I am here, I will take your burdens upon me; I will take your pain and bear it, and I will die on your behalf so that life for you will be forever. That is why I was born."

Jesus spoke with power; so much so that, for a moment, his words stilled the noise and the commotion in the great metropolitan center.

■ *"Come to me...all who are weary..."*

14th Sunday in Ordinary Time (A)   *Matthew 11:25-30*

Most people do not recall their first experience with either of their parents. Some very few do!

Listen to a privileged experience:

There was a woman of fifty-five years who came to an orphanage to take a child of twelve to her home—to his new home.

Neither had ever met before. The youngster had been informed earlier in the morning of this impending adoption, of which he knew the ramifications only vaguely. Even the practical implications of
new friends,
new school,
new neighborhood,
and a whole
new world weren't discussed nor ever mentioned to him.

Later that morning, the woman and the young boy
met for the first time. Very little was spoken; both
were extremely nervous. Smiles were there, of
course, but "What is this all about?" was heavy in
the boy's gut.

At noontime the woman and lad were driving home
on one of the
        biggest,
        busiest
thoroughfares in Philadelphia. Still, few words were
exchanged between them; both were even more ap-
prehensive than before.

Suddenly the woman's car hit the curb of the left-
hand island, which spun the vehicle to the righthand
island, which set the vehicle wheeling out of control
and hitting both islands several more times.

As the car came to a screeching halt, the brakes
finally taking hold, the woman looked apologetically
at the youngster, and he at her with trepidation.
They just looked at one another. No words could
possibly suffice. They both instinctively knew that
        the road,
        the journey
from then on would be a
        bumpy,
        rocky one indeed.
And it was.

But
        bumpy,
        rocky

          roads,
          journeys
are not all bad.

In truth, rocky journeys can be surprisingly good and challenging.

What rocky journeys do is force people to invite Jesus into their lives.
          The woman,
          the young boy
did. They had to! Their approaches were different, but the son learned from the mother a steadfast loyalty to the Master.

The woman knew Jesus so well that she boldly took the Master at his word, "Come to me, all you who are weary and find life burdensome..."—but not before she showed her stubborn independence!

Years later, when the woman's husband died, a man who was indeed her best friend, she was beside herself. Jesus, sensing this, came to her asking if she would feel better in paradise with George. The woman politely replied:

"No, everything will be OK. I appreciate your offer, and I love you very much, and I will continue to pray to you for comfort, but really, I'm all right, Jesus."

Jesus was puzzled, "Are you sure, Anna?"

"Certainly! Now don't be pushy," said she. "I will call you when things become too much, I've got

traveling to do,
cards to play,
Senior Citizens to join,
Ladies' Auxiliary to serve—
scram now!"

Jesus knew when to back off and left!

Another time Jesus met the woman at the local
hospital before she was to undergo major surgery at
the age of 78. Jesus held her hand, "Anna, are you
ready to come to me?" The woman
smiled faintly,
answered firmly,
"Not yet, Jesus. Things are
hectic and
tiresome, even
burdensome,
but I can still hack it, now shoo! Don't be a pest. I'll
be OK. I love you,
I'll be able to handle things.
I'll let you know otherwise."

Last Tuesday morning, though very weak, the
woman went grocery shopping. Standing across the
street stood Jesus as she came out of the store.
Though
her eyes were tired,
her legs sore,
her arms weak,
her back giving out,
she spotted Jesus, and tears flowed willingly. The
Master beckoned the woman to come to him. She approached Jesus and said, "I feel terribly burdened.
Lord,

I'm weary,
I'm tired,
I'm ready to go with you now."
Jesus opened his arms wide, and as he did so, the woman thrust her grocery bag to his chest and told the Master to meet her at the hospital in an hour or so, "'cause I'm going home to take care of some final business."

I can vouch for the authenticity of this story: the woman was my mother. I mentioned at my mom's funeral that she knew the fullness of reconciliation and discipleship before dying. Shortly before my mom died, she wrote on a piece of paper the following:

...instead of flowers and Mass cards, I ask money be given to the charity of my son's choosing...

This was gratifying to me simply because though
flowers are nice and
Mass cards important,
my mom knew Jesus well enough to know the moneys given could be better spent on giving nourishment to his needy and poor. In doing this, my mom moved the attention from her to the poor, who really need it! And that is truly the fullness of discipleship.
Thank you, mom.
I love you.
Godspeed Forever,
Lou.

■ Index of Scripture References

More Storytelling In Ministry Ideas!

NO KIDDING, GOD, WHERE ARE YOU?
Parables of Ordinary Experience
Lou Ruoff
Paperbound $7.95, 106 pages, 5½" x 8½", ISBN 0-89390-141-5
See how Gospels come alive in today's most enthusiastic language and symbols. In his first collection of stories, this gifted storyteller helps reveal God to those who sometimes feel that God is hiding. These 25 stories work as effective homilies and are great for your planning — they are accompanied by both Scripture and lectionary references.

PARABLES OF BELONGING:
Discipleship and Commitment in Everyday Life
Lou Ruoff
Paperbound $8.95, 112 pages, 5½" x 8½", ISBN 0-89390-253-5
This collection of stories recognizes the ability of average people to minister to others in their lives just by carrying out their day-to-day activities. Telling these stories will help listeners acknowledge and rejoice in their own "hidden" giftedness.

THE MAGIC STONE and Other Stories for the Faith Journey
James L. Henderschedt
Paperbound $7.95, 95 pages, 5½" x 8½", ISBN 0-89390-116-4
Put Scripture in context with today's lifestyles and the word becomes reality for you. Share it aloud and the word comes to life for your congregation, prayer group, or adult education class. These stories invite readers and listeners alike to think about the "moral" of the story, about the story's significance in their lives, and about how this story can help their spiritual growth.

THE TOPSY-TURVY KINGDOM: More Stories for Your Faith Journey
James L. Henderschedt
Paperbound $7.95, 122 pages, 5½" x 8½", ISBN 0-89390-177-6
Twenty-one stories that turn the ordinary world upside down and inside out. Use them for preaching — they're keyed to the lectionary — or use them in religious education. Your listeners will see themselves in the characters Henderschedt paints so vividly — perhaps in Jason, the bully from the title story, or in the two frail young people in "The Dance."

THE LIGHT IN THE LANTERN: True Stories for Your Faith Journey
James L. Henderschedt
Paperbound $8.95, 124 pages, 5½" x 8½", ISBN 0-89390-209-8
This collection, linked to the lectionary, goes beyond facts to the "truth" of one's faith journey. Use these stories for personal reflection, homily preparation, or small group work.

Order from your local bookseller or use the order form on the last page.

More Storytelling In Ministry Ideas!

STORIES TO INVITE FAITH-SHARING:
Experiencing the Lord through the Seasons
Mary McEntee McGill
Paperbound $8.95, 128 pages, 5½" x 8½", ISBN 0-89390-230-6
These twenty stories, based on real life experiences, can help us recognize God's presence in everyday life. Reflections and questions for group sharing can lead to personal awareness and prayer. Great for faith-sharing groups, workshops, and retreats.

STORIES FOR CHRISTIAN INITIATION
Joseph J. Juknialis
Paperbound $8.95, 152 pages, 6" x 9", ISBN 0-89390-235-7
Organized around the adult catechumenate, these imaginative stories resonate with key lectionary passages and stages of the catechumenate Great for generating discussions. Reflections, questions, and rituals for each story will help catechumens tell their own stories.

A STILLNESS WITHOUT SHADOWS
Joseph J. Juknialis
Paperbound $7.95, 75 pages, 6" x 9", ISBN 0-89390-081-8
This collection contains 13 stories, including: "The Cup," "The Golden Dove," "Bread that Remembers," "Golden Apples," "Pebbles at the Wall," and "Lady of the Grand." You'll find an appendix that tells you how to use the stories in church, school, or home.

WHEN GOD BEGAN IN THE MIDDLE
Joseph J. Juknialis
Paperbound $7.95, 101 pages, 6" x 9", ISBN 0-89390-027-3
In this collection of stories, find out what lies "Twixt Spring and Autumn" and "Why Water Lost Her Color." Meet Greta and Andy, whose mountain is "Carved Out of Love."

WINTER DREAMS and Other Such Friendly Dragons
Joseph J. Juknialis
Paperbound $7.95, 87 pages, 6" x 9", ISBN 0-89390-010-9
This book of dramas, fairly tales, and fables dances with images that spark into clarity old and treasured principles. Discover the blessings concealed in "If Not For Our Unicorns" and "In Search of God's Tracks."

Order from your local bookseller or use the order form on the last pag

Stories for Working with Children

PARABLES FOR LITTLE PEOPLE
Lawrence Castagnola, SJ
Paperbound $7.95, 101 pages, 5½" x 8½", ISBN 0-89390-034-6
Be forewarned. When you pick up these stories, you risk being transformed. The language of children relays the message of these 16 powerful parables. Castagnola artfully reaches children in preaching, in teaching, and in the simple pleasures of storytelling.

MORE PARABLES FOR LITTLE PEOPLE
Lawrence Castagnola, SJ
Paperbound $8.95, 100 pages, 5½" x 8½", ISBN 0-89390-095-8
Enjoy this companion volume to *Parables for Little People*. It gives you 15 imaginative children's stories with happy, positive messages. Find seven stories concerning the gospel themes of sharing, caring, non-violence, and women's rights. Discover still other stories that retell Gospel stories — without mentioning the names of the original characters.

TELLING STORIES LIKE JESUS DID:
Creative Parables for Teachers
Christelle L. Estrada
Paperbound $8.95, 100 pages, 5½" x 8½", ISBN 0-89390-097-4
Bring home the heart of Jesus' message by personalizing the parables of Luke. Each chapter includes introductory comments and questions, an easy-to-use storyline, and discussion questions for primary, intermediate, and junior high grades.

BALLOONS! CANDY! TOYS!
and Other Parables for Storytellers
Daryl Olszewski
Paperbound $8.95, 100 pages, 5½" x 8½", ISBN 0-89390-069-9
Learn how to make stories into faith experiences for children and adults. Learn to tell about "An Evening With Jesus" and "From Hostility to Hospitality". Nine delightful parables plus commentary that shows readers how to tell the stories, how to use them in preaching and teaching, and how to come up with new stories.

ANGELS TO WISH BY: A Book of Story-Prayers
Joseph J. Juknialis
Paperbound $7.95, 136 pages, 6" x 9", ISBN 0-89390-051-6
A delight to read as a collection of stories as well as a book well suited for use in preparing liturgies. Scripture references, prayers, and activities that show how these story-prayers can be put to practical use in your parish situation accompany most of the stories.

Order from your local bookseller or use the order form on the last page.

Stories for Growth and Change

WHO KILLED STUTZ BEARCAT?: Stories of Finding Faith after Loss
Kristen Johnson Ingram
Paperbound $8.95, 96 pages, 5½" x 8½", ISBN 0-89390-264-0
Nine stories confront losses head-on and reveal resurrection experiences. Reflection questions will lead readers beyond the author's stories into their own and, ultimately, to a better understanding of the paschal mystery. This book is appropriate for pastoral counseling, individual reflection, or transition and grief groups.

BREAKTHROUGH: Stories of Conversion
Andre Papineau
Paperbound $7.95, 139 pages, 5½" x 8½", ISBN 0-89390-128-8
Here is an essential resource for catechumenate, Cursillo, and renewal programs. Witness what takes place inside Papineau's characters as they change, and learn that change, ultimately, is a positive experience. You'll find reflections from a psychological point of view following each section to help you to help others deal with their personal conversions.

JESUS ON THE MEND: Healing Stories for Ordinary People
Andre Papineau
Paperbound $7.95, 150 pages, 5½" x 8½", ISBN 0-89390-140-7
Better understand healing, so that you, like Jesus, can bring comfort to those who hurt. Here are 18 Gospel-based stories that illustrate four aspects of healing: Acknowledging the Need, Reaching Out for Help, The Healer's Credentials, and The Healer's Therapy. Also includes helpful reflections following each story, focusing on the process of healing that takes place.

BIBLICAL BLUES: Growing Through Setups and Letdowns
Andre Papineau
Paperbound $7.95, 226 pages, 5½" x 8½", ISBN 0-89390-157-1
Be transformed while you are deep into your own personal recovery. This book of biblical stories acknowledges the way people set themselves up for a letdown to come later. Papineau consoles us in revealing that Jesus, ever the playful one, often enters the scene to puncture a balloon, a deflating event that somehow leads to spiritual growth.

Order Form

Order these resources from your local bookstore, or mail this form to:

QTY	TITLE	PRICE	TOTAL

Subtotal: _____

CA residents add 7¼% sales tax
(Santa Clara Co. residents, 8¼%): _____

Postage and handling
($2 for order up to $20; 10% of order over $20 but less than $150; $15 for order of $150 or more): _____

Total: _____

Resource Publications, Inc.
160 E. Virginia Street #290 - FG
San Jose, CA 95112-5876
(408) 286-8505
(408) 287-8748 FAX

☐ My check or money order is enclosed.
☐ Charge my ☐ VISA ☐ MC.
Expiration Date _____
Card # _____ - _____ - _____ - _____
Signature _____
Name (print) _____
Institution _____
Street _____
City/State/ZIP _____